ISBN 978-0-260-57318-6
PIBN 10957025

ANNUAL CATALOG

OF

STATE NORMAL SCHOOL

ST. CLOUD, MINN.

FOR THE

SCHOOL YEAR ENDING MAY 29, 1912 .

WITH

ANNUAL ANNOUNCEMENT

FOR THE YEAR 1912-1913

STATE NORMAL SCHOOL

FACULTY OF INSTRUCTION

W. A. SHOEMAKER, Pd. D., President,
    Methods and School Economy.

ISABEL LAWRENCE,
    Psychology, Methods and Superintendent of Training School.

GEO. C. HUBBARD, B. S.,
    Biological Science.

***P. M. MAGNUSSON, Ph. D.,
    History, Civics and Sociology.

P. P. COLGROVE, Pd. D.,
    Mathematics, and Science of Education.

IVER T. JOHNSRUD, B. A.,
    Physical Science and Mathematics.

ELSPA MILLICENT DOPP, M. L.,
    Literature.

*LULA MARGARET PALMER, A. B.,
    Latin.

*FRANCES O. CRAVENS, A. B.,
    Reading.

PAPE L. QUAYLE, A. B.,
    Grammar.

**CLARA L. STILES, B. S.,
    Geography.

CARRIE E. MINICH,
    Drawing.

ADA BICKING,
    Music.

JULIA BOOTH,
    Expression.

CARRIE BARDEN, M. A.,
    Composition.

**KATE KENELY,
    History, Civics and Sociology.

EVALIN PRIBBLE, B. S.,
    Composition.

HELEN BALLY, Ph. B.,
    Geography and Botany.

**MYRTLE OLIVER, A. B.,
    Mathematics and History.

BLANCHE ATKINS, Ph. B.,
    Methods.

LEONARD A. WILLIAMS.
    Manual Training.

ANNA E. SMITH,
    Domestic Science.

JOSEPHINE V. BROWER,
    Physical Culture.

GEORGE LYNCH,
    Physical Culture and Director of Athletics.

RUTH CROSSMAN,
    Sewing.

NATHANIEL QUICKSTAD,
    Assistant in Physical Science.

FRANK S. ELRICK,
    Assistant in Manual Training.

**ISABEL O. SHOEMAKER,
    Mathematics and Reading.

***MARY NICHOLAS,
    History.

DARIUS STEWARD, B. A.,
    Critic in Training School, Departmental.

***JESSIE BURRALL,
    Critic in Training School, Eighth Grade.

ALBERTINA C. ANDERSON,
    Critic in Training School, Sixth and Seventh Grades.

M. GERTRUDE FLYNN, B. S.,
    Critic in Training School, Fourth and Fifth Grades.

BEULAH DOUGLAS,
    Critic in Training School, Primary Grades.

RENA J. BRUCE,
    Critic in Training School, Departmental.

ANNE HITCHCOCK,
    Critic in Training School, Departmental.

**CORDELIA ESSLING,
    Critic in Training School, Eighth Grade.

GEORGIA VADEBONCOEUR,
    Critic in Training School, Music.

GERTRUDE CAMBELL,
    Librarian.

MABEL LYONS,
    Assistant Librarian.

MARY CRAIK-PERCY,
    Stenographer.

ELLEN READY,
    Matron and Preceptress of Lawrence Hall.

ANNA ALDEN,
    Office Assistant.

*Away on leave of absence for year.

**Away on leave of absence for one term.

***Away on leave of absence for two terms.

CALENDAR

SUMMER TERM

Term opens.................................Tuesday, June 11, 1912

Term ends.............................Friday noon, July 26, 1912

FALL TERM

Term opens................................Tuesday, Sept. 10, 1912.

Fall term ends at 10:10 a. m.............Wednesday, Nov. 27, 1912

WINTER TERM

Class work begins..........................Tuesday, Dec. 3, 1912

Holiday vacation begins at 10:10.............Friday, Dec. 20, 1912

School reopens..............................Tuesday, Jan. 7, 1913

Winter term ends..........................Friday, March 7, 1913

SPRING TERM

Class work begins........................Monday, March 10, 1913

Easter vacation begins at 10:10 a. m.....Wednesday, March 19, 1913

School reopens...........................Tuesday, March 25, 1913

Spring term ends.............................Friday, June 6, 1913

CIRCULAR

THE PURPOSE OF THE SCHOOL

The aim of this school is to qualify young people for the teaching service of the State of Minnesota. To the extent that the purpose of an organization determines its character, all the work of the school is professional. It does not give general culture for its own sake. It does not aim to prepare young men and women for college nor for the general pursuits of life. The school does not give general culture. Those who complete its full course, are given two years' credit at the State University. Professional work upon the common school branches and other subjects includes a preparation for business. The moral education which qualifies young men and women to be safe guides for the state's children is a good preparation for "complete living," and is beneficial in all walks of life. These results, however, though actual and abundant, are incidental to the primary purpose of the school.

The constantly increasing demand for better schools gives rise to an urgent demand for more teachers who have received adequate training and preparation for their work. It is the special function of the Normal School to supply this demand.

ENTRANCE REQUIREMENTS

1. A second grade certificate, or credits admitting to a high school course or the equivalent, will admit a student without examination.

While graduates of the eighth grade will be admitted, such admissions will be limited to those whose records and maturity indicate the ability to carry the work.

Examinations will be held on the first day, for those who do not have the necessary credentials.

Students must pass examination in the subjects of Arithmetic, Grammar, Geography and United States History. They are expected to have a thorough knowledge of the subjects named as presented in the larger editions of the current leading modern text books.

In Reading, they are to show ability to read at sight, intelligently and fluently, ordinary, easy prose and simple poetry; and in Composition, the ability to write a simple essay correctly and in proper form.

2. High school graduates should present the diploma from a four years' high school course and high school standings. For the full course, this is all that is necessary.

For an elementary diploma at the end of one year, High School Graduates should present standings in Botany or Zoology, Chemistry or Physics, Civics and United States History studied in the high school. If these standings are not included in the credits presented, the student will be conditioned, and must take them in the normal school in addition to the subjects of his course.

3. High school graduates who shall have taken, as post graduate work, at least a half-year's work in Normal subjects as offered in state high schools, may receive credit for subjects in which they shall have done a full semester's work; provided (1) that these credits apply only on the two years' graduate course; (2) that the president reserves the right to test the quality of the work, and (3) that the maximum amount of credit given shall be limited to one-half year.

4. A first grade certificate valid at the time of presentation, entitles its holder to twelve credits on the course; provided (1) that the subjects to be credited shall be designated by the president, and (2) that the average of the certificates is not less than 75 per cent and that subjects in which the standings are less than 75 per cent are not credited, and that the number of credits allowed be proportionately reduced.

THE COURSE OF STUDY FOR MINNESOTA NORMAL SCHOOLS

(Adopted September 18, 1908)

For detailed information respecting the subjects, the reader is referred to the Synopsis of the Course of Study which appears on subsequent pages.

Algebra, I, II, III.
Arithmetic, I, II, III.
Botany, I, II.
Chemistry, I, II.
Civics, I, II, III.
Drawing, I, II, III.
Education.
    History of, I, II.
    Theory of, I, II.
    Practice of, I, II, III.
    School Management, ½.
Elem. Science, 1.
English Composition, I, II.
Geography, I, II, III, IV.
Geometry, I, II, III.
Grammar, I, II, III, IV.

History, U. S., I, II, III.
History, General, I, II, III.
History, English, I.
Latin, I XI.
Literature, I, II, III, IV.
Manual Training, I, II, III.
Music, I, II, III.
Physics, I, II, III.
Physiography, I.
Physiology, I.
Psychology, I, II.
Reading and Expres'n, I. II, III, IV.
Rhetoric, I.
Social Science, I.
Themes, I.
Zoology, I, II.

ELECTIVES

+ As the facilities of the schools permit, one or more of the following electives will be offered, and may be chosen by the student, after consultation with the president, in lieu of starred subjects in the course of study.

Agriculture, I, II.
Advanced Physics, I.
Astronomy, I.
Children's Literature, I.
Drawing Supervision, I, II.
Economics, I.
English, VIII, IX.
Home Economics, I, II, III.
Higher Mathematics, I, II.
Latin, XII, XIII.

Library Science, I.
Manual Training, IV, V.
Modern Europ. Hist., I, II.
Music Supervision, I, II.
Physical Culture, I.
Primary Methods, I.
Public Speaking, I.
Special Methods, I.
Writing & Spelling, ½.

COURSE OF STUDY BY YEARS AND TERMS

Note—The program for a given term includes many subjects not listed for that term.

FIRST YEAR

First	Second	Third
* Arith. 1	* Arith. 2	* Eng. Comp. 2
* Read. 1	* (Gram. 1	* (Gram. 2
	(Latin 2	(Latin 3
* (Eng. Comp. 1	* Geog. 1	* Geog. 2
(Latin 1	* Draw. 1	* Physiology
* Music 1		

SECOND YEAR

First	Second	Third
* Alg. 1	* Alg. 2	* Alg. 3
* Bot. 1	* (Bot. 2	(Lat. 6
* Music 2	(Latin 5	* (Zool. 1
* (Eng. Hist.	* Hist., U. S. 1	* Hist., U. S. 2
(Latin 4	* Geom. 1	* Geom. 2

THIRD YEAR

First	Second	Third
* Physics 1	* Physics 2	(Physics 3
* (Rhet.	* Lit. 1	* (Psychology 1
(Latin 7	* Draw. 2	* (Lit. 2
* Read. 2	(Zool. 2	(Latin 8
(Zool. 1	(Eng. Hist. (Lat.	* Civics
* (Gen. Meth. 1 (30)	Students.	(Elective
* (Meth. Read. 1 (30)	* (Teaching 1	* (Teaching 2

FOURTH YEAR

First	Second	Third
(Domestic Science	(Astronomy	Physiography
(Chem. 1	(Chem. 2	(Gen. Hist. 3
(Latin 9		(H. S. Gram. Latin
Gen. Hist. 1	Gen. Hist. 2	Students.
(Gen. Meth. 1 (30)	(Geom. 3	(Man. Tr. 1
(Meth. Read. 1 (30)	(Latin 10	(Latin 11
Expression	Psychology 1	Meth. Ad. or Pri.

    * For elementary diploma.

FIFTH YEAR

First	Second	Third
Psychology 2	Social Science	Lit. 4
Teaching 1	Lit. 3	Child Study
Teaching 2	His. of Educ.	Man. Tr. 2
Criticism	Themes	* (School Man. ½
		(Elective ½

High School Graduate Course

FIRST YEAR

First	Second	Third
(Gen. Meth. 1 (30)	(Gen. Meth. 2 (30)	Psychology 1
(Meth. Read. 1 (30)	(Meth. Read. 2 (30)	
Meth. Gram.	Meth. Geog.	El. Sci.
Music	Drawing	(Meth. Ad. or Pri.
		* (Teaching 2
Meth. Arith.	(Meth. Hist.	Expression
	* (Teaching 1	* Phys. Cul.

SECOND YEAR

First	Second	Third
Psychology 2	Social Science	Lit. 4
Teaching 1	Hist. of Educ.	Child Study
Teaching 2	Themes	* (School Man. ½
Criticism	Man. Tr.	(Elective ½
		Physiography

Note—For elementary diploma subjects marked * must be substituted in first year.

At the meeting of the State Normal Board on February 14th, 1911, the following courses were adopted:—

I. **Manual Training and Drawing.**

In addition to the two years of the present course as stated:

3 units. Shop work.

3 units. Drawing.

2 units. Either drawing or manual training.

1 unit. Teaching.

1 unit. History and organization.

2 units. Electives (if special electives were taken in first two years; if they were not, then 2 units of special work are to be added here.)

Minimum, 8 technical units in one subject.

II. Cooking and Sewing.

In addition to the two years' course:

3 units. Cooking.

3 units. Sewing.

1 unit. Chemistry and Bacteriology.

1 unit. Physiology and Hygiene.

1 unit. Teaching.

1 unit. Drawing and Design.

2 units. Elective (if special electives were taken in first two years.)

Minimum, 10 units of Professional Work for diploma.

Condition of admission, Chemistry ½ year in high school or one term in Normal school.

On May 6th, 1911, the following special courses for elementary school supervisors were adopted:

Professional Subjects.................................Three terms.
Principals of education, school administration, course of study, observation, supervision and criticism.

Academic Subjects ....Three terms.
Higher courses in literature, history, science, mathematics, industrial or art subjects.

Electives ....Three terms.
Subjects such as education, geography, mathematics, English, history, etc., for those preparing to do departmental work or other work of special character, provided that the choice shall lie in at least two fields of study.

Thesis ....One term.
An exhaustive investigation in and a written report on an approved phase of education.

LEGAL FORCE OF DIPLOMAS

Act of Legislature, April 21, 1909

"Diplomas issued to graduates of the State Normal Schools****
shall be valid as first grade certificates for two years from their
date, and at the expiration of two years of actual, successful teaching
such diplomas, endorsed by the president of the school granting them,
and the state superintendent, shall have force of first grade certificates for life.

"Elementary diplomas granted by a State Normal school upon
the completion of such portion of the course of study as may be
prescribed therefore by the Normal School Board shall be valid as
first grade certificates for a period of three years from their date,
and shall not be renewable; except that any holder of such an
elementary diploma may have the force and effect thereof, as such
first grade certificate, extended for a further period of three years
by the completion of an additional one year of work in a Minnesota
State Normal school, and the certificate of indorsement thereon by
the president of such school and the state superintendent; provided,
that the provisions of this section shall not apply to persons now
holding Minnesota elementary Normal school diplomas nor to any
student heretofore enrolled in a Minnesota State Normal school who
shall be graduated prior to September 1, 1911.

"The holders of certificates from the State Normal schools show-
ing the completion of two years of prescribed work in such schools
shall be entitled to have such certificates endorsed by the superintendent of public instruction and thereby given the full force and
effect of a second grade certificate."

Conditions of Endorsement

1. While it is hoped that all graduates will earn the right to
have their diplomas endorsed, great care will be taken in this matter,
and the indorsement will not be granted in any case in which the
holder fails to render acceptable service during the test period, or
in any way fails to show himself worthy of the marked professional
recognition and honor so bestowed.

2. After the completion of two years of service, application for
indorsement may be made to the respective Normal Schools, upon
blanks furnished for that purpose. The applicant should make a

complete report of teaching done since graduation, and should give the names and addresses of the supervising school authorities under whom the work was done, and to whom blanks may be sent upon which to give their testimonials as to the quality of the service rendered. When such testimonials have been received, if they are approved by the Board of Presidents of Normal Schools, a certificate of indorsement will be sent to the applicant.

THE VALUE OF COMPLETING THE FULL COURSE

Aside from the culture gained, the following advantages result from completing the full course:

1. It insures a life certificate in this state, after two years of successful teaching, while diplomas for part work cannot be endorsed.

2. The diploma of the full course is the only one honored in most other states.

3. High school graduates who have many conditions to make up, must stay four terms to gain an elementary diploma, while six terms would bring the advanced.

4. Students who have had two years or more of work in high schools without graduation, cannot obtain the elementary three years' diploma without remaining two years or more in the Normal school. They often have, however, enough advanced credits to give them the diploma of the full course, if they remain but one year longer, or three years.

The University of Minnesota on April 26, 1911, made the following ruling: That a graduate from a four-year high school, who shall have completed the full two years' course in a Minnesota State Normal School and shall be recommended by the president of the Normal School from which he has graduated, shall be granted in the University a sufficient number of credits so that the four years' course, leading to the degree of B. A. in Education, may be completed in two years.

SESSIONS OF THE SCHOOL

There are five daily sessions of the school each week, from 8:30 a. m. to 4 p. m.

The evening hours of study are from 7:00 to 9:00 o'clock p. m., daily, except on Friday and Saturday evenings. This arrangement divides the day into two periods; that from 8:30 a. m. to 4:00 p. m.

during which time the students are engaged principally in recitations, and that covered by the study hours in the evening. The strict
observance of the latter period is of quite as much importance as
the former. No pupil will be expected to absent himself from duty
during either interval, nor will it be presumed that pupils are to be
interrupted by callers or visitors during their study hours, any more
than during the hours of recitation. As the spirit of the school is
thoroughly loyal to this plan, any person feeling himself unable to
comply cheerfully with these habits of work will not find the school
congenial.

ADMISSION

1. Students whose health is not good, should not attempt to
enter upon a Normal School course. A person with any physical
defects, should select any occupation rather than that of a teacher.

2. A teacher must be able to use clear and correct language
both oral and written. Students who fail in this respect, will be
required to take English composition even though they have passing
standings in the subject given here or elsewhere.

3. Students must sign a pledge to teach two years in the
schools of the state, unless prevented by circumstances beyond their
control, and to report semi-annually to the President.

4. Graduates of high schools and colleges will be passed in
subjects other than professional, without examination, on the certificate of the Principal that they have already completed these subjects with a grade of not less than 75 per cent.

5. Term credits will be given to those taking the full course,
for post graduate normal review work done in the State High schools,
provided that such standings from High Schools represent a full
semester's work. The Normal faculty reserves the right to test the
scope of such review work. Maximum amount of credit allowed for
such work done in High Schools is limited to one-half year's work.

6. Students will not be received after the beginning of a term
except upon the most satisfactory excuse. Any who cannot be
present upon the first day of the term should report to the President
beforehand, that their absence may be understood. It is not expected
that students will leave before the close of the term unless com-
pelled to do so by circumstances beyond their control.

7. Students arranging their programs should remember that psychology, general methods and practice must not be taken simultaneously, but must follow in sequence taking not less than three terms.

SUGGESTIONS TO APPLICANTS

Obtain a letter from your County Superintendent, if possible, introducing you to some member of the faculty of the school. This will be all the recommendation you will need.

Bring with you your credits, diploma, certificates from High school board, state teachers' certificates and all standings beyond the eighth grade. The school furnishes a blank on which such standings may be entered.

Students will be transferred from one State Normal school to another, only upon written permission granted by the President of the State Normal Board.

Credits for University work, or work in other colleges or Normal schools will be given on our course, but a minimum of one year's resident work will in all cases be required for graduation.

Students must come fully prepared to give their undivided attention to the work of the school during the entire term. The demands ·of the school are so pressing that the students cannot be permitted to engage during the term in any employment or pleasure —as taking private music lessons, or attending parties or entertainments—which is not directly connected with their work.

LIBRARY

A library of several thousand volumes is open to the school. A full supply of the standard reference books, dictionaries, encyclopaedias, gazeteers, etc., furnish all needed information upon subjects discussed in the classroom.

A library of text books upon all topics is open to the students, where they can find help in examining the various methods presented by our standard text-book authors in the different branches.

This school has been designated as a depository of public documents, and now has on its shelves over 3,000 volumes from the government printing office, many of them of great value. They are open to the public for consultation at any time during the day from 8:30 a. m. to 4:30 p. m.

READING ROOM

The reading room contains a large list of the leading newspapers, magazines and educational periodicals.

DOMESTIC SCIENCE ROOM

PRACTICE CLASS, PRIMARY DEPARTMENT

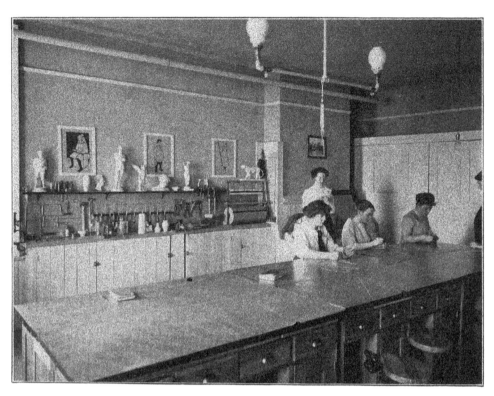

ELEMENTARY MANUAL ARTS ROOM

SEWING ROOM

Both the reading room and library are open daily to students during the hours of the day when they are not required to attend to the other duties of the school.

LITERARY SOCIETIES

The Normal Literary Societies furnish excellent opportunities for social and literary culture, and all students are advised to become active members.

BOARDING

General Regulations

Particular attention is called to the following points:

1. Students who do not board at home are expected to consult the President before selecting boarding places.

2. Ladies and gentlemen will not be permitted to board in the same family. This rule shall apply equally where the house is occupied by two or more families.

3. Permission must be obtained in every case where pupils desire to board with families where boarders are taken who are not connected with the school.

4. Brothers and sisters will be allowed to board in the same house provided no other boarders are received into the house.

5. Students will not be expected to change their boarding places without consulting the President.

6. When students engage a boarding place, it will be understood that they are to remain in that place until the end of the current term, unless a specific bargain to the contrary is made.

7. Every means will be taken to secure suitable boarding places for such students as desire this service, and families in which students board will be encouraged to report the least departure from perfectly ladylike and gentlemanly conduct.

8. Pupils are not expected to receive calls during study hours.

LAWRENCE HALL

The dormitory known as Lawrence Hall is an invaluable adjunct to the school. The nearness of the hall to the school makes it peculiarly desirable during the winter months, saving a long walk through the cold and snow.

The hall is furnished with electric lights throughout and supplied with every convenience of the best modern homes. Large bath rooms, supplied with hot and cold water, are located on each floor.

The comfort and convenience of young ladies at the hall has been made a matter of long and careful study, and it can be confidently said that it affords to those so fortunate as to live there all pleasures of a home with none of the discomforts of a boarding house. The house is furnished throughout with new and substantial furniture.

Rooms for students are supplied with table, chairs, rugs, two bedsteads, springs, mattress, pillows, bureau, commode, washbowl and pitcher, window shades, napkins, towels, pillow cases, sheets, two blankets, comfortables, and spreads, and every room has two closets. Each young lady is requested to bring a waterproof cloak, umbrella and a pair of rubbers.

Students boarding at the hall are required to do no work under the present management, excepting that they take turns in waiting upon the table.

The supervision of the establishment is in the hands of a competent matron who devotes her entire time and attention to securing the physical and social comfort of the young ladies.

Such rates of boarding as this school affords, it is firmly believed, cannot be excelled by any other school in the country.

The price per week, including furnished room, light, fuel, board, use of laundry, bath rooms and all conveniences of the hall, is three dollars and twenty-five cents ($3.25)—payable monthly in advance. The price per week is four dollars ($4.00) if one person occupies a room alone. Table board without room is two dollars and fifty cents ($2.50) per week.

While most of the washing is done by steam laundries in the city, a limited amount may be done by the young ladies in the hall laundry. All the ironing may be done by the students if they so desire.

Preference in choice of rooms will be given in the order of application. Rooms are engaged by the term. Those wishing to occupy them for a shorter time should notify the matron of the fact at the time of engaging them.

Board can be secured in private families at from $3.25 to $4.00 per week.

TUITION

Tuition is free to all students who enter the Normal department and sign the required pledge to teach two years in the public schools of the state.

To all not so pledged to teach, the tuition is $10 per term.

All tuition is payable by terms, strictly in advance, and no portion of the amount will be refunded.

TEXT BOOKS

Text books are furnished free of charge to all who pay tuition; other students pay a uniform fee of $1.50 per term for the rental of all text books needed.

In the Model School the charge for book rent varies from twenty cents per term in the second grade to eighty cents per term in the eighth grade.

A strict account is kept of any injury done to books and a charge made therefor.

Students are allowed to purchase their books if they prefer to do so. To these students, books are sold at the lowest wholesale rates.

HOW TO REACH THE SCHOOL

If south of St. Paul or Minneapolis, buy your ticket to either one of these cities, and there purchase over the Great Northern or Northern Pacific road, a ticket to St. Cloud. Upon reaching the station take an omnibus and tell the driver to take you to the Normal School. Upon arriving, report to the President at his office.

ORCHESTRA

An orchestra is maintained in connection with the music department.

It is desired that those who play instruments should bring them from home. Opportunity will be offered to join the orchestra early in the year.

GENERAL REMARKS

It is to be hoped that County and City Superintendents, Principals, Teachers and other friends of the Normal School will be ready to advise those who are striving to make themselves good teachers, to enter some department of the school.

School Superintendents and all other friends of education are earnestly invited to visit and inspect the workings of this school, and by their criticism, suggestion and co-operation, aid us in supplying the schools of the state with better-trained teachers.

Address letters of inquiry and requests for catalogues to the

PRESIDENT, State Normal School,

St. Cloud, Minn.

SUBJECTS OF THE COURSE

METHOD

One term is devoted to the general principles of teaching, observation of lessons, and lesson planning. A second term is given specifically to primary work, or advanced work, as the student may elect.

PRACTICE

Students spend 24 weeks in practice, one hour per day. They teach in this time four different classes, in four different subjects six weeks each. One of these classes is an entire grade in the city schools of St. Cloud.

PSYCHOLOGY

During the first term of psychology, the student is lead to observe the workings of his own mind, and to become acquainted with the language of the subject.

During the second term, more analysis is attempted. Emotions are quite thoroughly studied with the basis of ethics.

The third term is devoted to child psychology.

ARITHMETIC

The holder of a second grade certificate, and the eighth grade graduate takes mensuration and common fractions the first term and decimal fractions and percentage the second term. High school graduates cover this entire field in one term. The amount of drill work which can be given varies according to the ability of the pupils. High school graduates need much less time for drill.

ALGEBRA

Students take algebra throughout the second year. What is usually regarded as elementary algebra including the fundamental processes, fractions, unknown quantities, and radicals comprises the work of the first two terms. Higher algebra including quadratics and progressions forms the work of the third term. Numerous supplementary texts are used for drill in both exercises and problems.

GEOMETRY

Plane geometry is taken the last two terms of the second year following about the same propositions for demonstration ordinarily found in text-books. The text used does not give the demonstrations but students are required to think out demonstrations from sugges- tions. Solid geometry is taken up in the same manner in the fourth year.

LITERATURE

Course I.—(a) Mythology.—Stories from classic myths and legends told in class.

Texts.—Gayley's Classic Myths, and Legends of King Arthur. Read Tennyson's Idylls of the King, Lowell's Vision of Sir Launfal, and Longfellow's Golden Legend.

Course I.—(b) Shakespeare.—Macbeth, Twelfth Night, Dramatiza- tion of stories.

Course II.—(a) Milton to Tennyson. (b) The Novel—Ivanhoe, Hypatia, etc.

Course III.—(a) American Literature.—Rapid reading of poets from Bryant to Holmes. Careful study of Pope, Whitman and Lanier. Topics upon authors from Irving to Van Dyke. (b) The Essay, from Bacon to Emerson.

Course IV.—(a) Browning and Tennyson. (b) Chaucer, The Folk Ballads, and the Illiad.

Theme-writing in connection with each course.

COMPOSITION

I. A review of capitalization and punctuation. Sentence structure.

II. Oral English. Short discussions—for personal expression. Correction of common errors of speech.

III. Written English. Themes, at least once a week. Letter- writing.

IV. English Classics. Uniform selections for the study of form, vocabulary, style. Home reading, assigned according to the special needs of individuals.

ENGLISH GRAMMAR

Aim: The first half of the course is given to the study of the sentence. The sentence is divided into its essential parts, modifiers, independent elements and connections.

During the second half of the course, parts of speech are studied as to classifications, inflections, and use.

LATIN

1st year.—Latin grammar. The text used is Hale's First Latin Book.

2nd year.—(a) Four books of Caesar's Gallic War; or, an equivalent amount from Miller and Beeson's Second Year Latin Book. (b) Latin composition based on the above, at least one period a week.

3rd year.—(a) Six of Cicero's orations. (b) Latin composition based on Cicero, one period a week.

4th year.—(a) Six books of Vergil's Aeneid. (b) Selections from Ovid.

In all four years a good deal of attention is paid to translating at sight.

HISTORY AND SOCIAL SCIENCE

General History—In which the emphasis is placed on modern history, as the period that comes in closest relation with our life today.

English History—In which the emphasis is placed on the development of popular self-government.

American History—In which we try to put the emphasis on organizing facts, not forgetting that teachers will find the story element especially useful in their own teaching.

History of Education—Which, besides being history, is used as a historical commentary on the science of teaching.

Methods in History—Is mainly a review of American history with the method of its teaching to children in view. In this course the pupils are also given the opportunity to get acquainted with classical historical literature for children.

Civics, Elementary Course—The principal object of this course is to give the pupil a working knowledge of our civic institutions. It is a sort of catechism in citizenship. The pupil is also introduced to the fundamental conceptions that underlie our civic life.

Civics, Advanced Course—Is a study of political (or civic) institutions and life with special reference to present-day problems.

Social Science—As taught here, is a study of the institutions of society, their evolution, and their present-day problems. Little attention is given to theory. The emphasis is placed on the study of live social problems.

PHYSICS

The work of the first term covers the subjects of physical properties of matter, laws of motion, force, work, simple machines—mechanics of solids and mechanics of fluids. The work of this term is made the basis of that which is to follow and must be taken before the work of either the second or the third term is attempted. The work of the second term, given in the winter term only, consists of a study of sound, magnetism, and electricity, while light and heat remain for the work of the third term. Either second or third term work may follow that of the first term.

Students must possess a good working knowledge of plane geometry and of elementary algebra through quadratics in order to do the work of the course intelligently.

ELEMENTARY SCIENCE

This is a course in applied science. The composition and structure of soils, water, air, vegetable and animal life are studied and the students are led to observe and understand what is going on in the world about them. The nature, cause and prevention of diseases of plants, animals and man receive some attention with special emphasis upon school sanitation and personal hygiene. To this end chemistry, physics, astronomy, botany, zoology, physiology, domestic science, agriculture and other sciences are drawn upon, and the relation of the facts of these sciences to organic life in general, and to the student's own life in particular, is made the subject matter of the course.

BOTANY

The instruction in this subject includes two recitations per week on plant organs and their functions, also eight hours per week in the laboratory studying plants as related to agriculture. In the spring and summer terms about two hours of the eight are spent in gardening. Each student attends to his own garden. Trees of the locality are studied, also many of the common shrubs and herbs. Attention is paid to weeds and their eradication. Considerable time is spent in the study of corn, wheat, oats, and other field crops. The course is twenty-four weeks in length.

ZOOLOGY

Two lessons per week are given over to leading zoological topics. The remaining eight hours are spent in the laboratory in work pertaining to common domestic animals. Field excursions are taken to gain acquaintance with common animals of field, forest, pond and stream. Attention is given to insects and birds in their relation to agriculture, in order to know which are beneficial and which detrimental. The subject continues throughout two terms.

PHYSIOLOGY

The principal organs and systems of the human body are studied, not so much for the purpose of learning their gross and histological structure, as to gain a knowledge of the laws governing health and physical vigor. The school is well supplied with the usual appliances for teaching this subject. The course continues for twelve weeks and is supplemented by lectures given by physicians of the city.

MUSIC

In this department the aim is two-fold. First. To give instruction in the rudiments and the method of teaching music. Second. To afford the culture which is gained by continued singing and hearing good music.

In the rudiments of music, instruction is given in sight reading, musical construction in its various phases, ear training, interpretation and voice culture.

An outline of methods in music, in which definite instructions for the teaching of music in all grades are laid down, is made by each student. Illustrative lessons are taught by student and instructor.

At chorus period daily and in special chorus standard compositions, choruses from the operas and oratorios are sung and students are trained in giving artistic interpretation and expression.

GEOGRAPHY

Course 1. Physical Geography—This course prepares one: (1) to see in the field and in the shops that which is essential to both political and commercial geography; (2) to recognize the great factors governing climate; (3) to express himself in good geographical language.

Course 2. Commercial Geography—(1) Type products with physical features which determine their location; (2) trade routes and trade centers.

Geography Methods—The work covers courses 1 and 2.

Physiography—(1) The origin of the physical features; (2) their adaptation to man.

DRAWING

This course includes free-hand drawing from nature and objects, also construction and design in the simplest forms. Pupils are taught to use all mediums suitable for public school work.

MANUAL ARTS COURSE

The following shop subjects require from 60 to 120 hours each per term of 12 weeks:

Mechanical Drawing, Architectural Drawing, Practice of Design, Woodwork I, II and III, Wood Burning and Pattern Making, Metal Work, Lettering and Printing, Bookbinding, Clay Modeling, Pottery, Weaving, Basketry, Cardboard Work, Paper Cutting, and Folding, Principles of Supervision and Methods. For information concerning advanced course in Manual Training see page 11.

DOMESTIC SCIENCE

The course in Domestic Science aims to make the student intelligent in the preparation of simple, wholesome food. The most important types of food are studied as to composition, digestibility and nutritive value. The principles underlying the cooking of these foods are determined by experimental work as far as practicable. Laboratory work is supplemented by lectures and reference work. During the course several meals are prepared and served as attractively as possible. The course requires one and one-half hours a day for one term. For information concerning advanced course in Home Economics, see course of study, page 12.

PHYSICAL CULTURE

Activities: School exercises, Calisthenics, Light Gymnastics with hand apparatus such as Indian Clubs, Bar Bells, Dumb Bells, Figure Marching, Gymnastic Games, such as Racing Games, Tag Games, All Up Relay, Shuttle Relay, Pass Ball Relay. Such Folk Dances and Folk Singing Games as have proved most useful.

The Folk Dances taught are selected from lists officially approved by the American Playground Association as suitable for indoors and out of doors, for small children, for larger boys, for larger girls, for adults, for various occupations, for special occasions.

ATHLETICS

The work in athletics has properly adjusted itself to the seasons, so that we now have football in the fall term, basketball in the winter term, and baseball in the spring term. In these games teams are trained to represent the institution and frequently make trips to other schools for the purpose of playing matched games. The department owns a full outfit of suits for these games and those who succeed in getting on the first team are supplied. Six tennis courts are now being built upon the campus. All students are eligible to play tennis and are given instruction in the art of the game. A tennis tournament is held during commencement week, in which the different classes are invited to participate. A silver cup is awarded to the winning class.

GYMNASTICS

A large gymnasium, well equipped with light American apparatus and with Swedish and German stationary apparatus, affords every opportunity for indoor exercise. Large rooms fitted up with lockers, dressing rooms and shower baths provided for the students who take part in gymnastics, are a valuable addition to the former equipment. All students from the first grade up are required to take physical training two periods a week. Measurements are taken at the beginning and at the end of the course, and prescriptions of suitable exercises made out for those who are not able to take the regular work. The work of the first year Normal classes is as follows:

(a) Fall term. Elementary Swedish gymnastics, games marching tactics, mat exercise and fancy steps.

(b) Winter term. Advanced Swedish gymnastics, games, tumbling, marching tactics and advanced fancy steps.

(c) Spring term. German gymnastics, advance marching tactics, theory of physical training with practical applications. This work is supplemented by the making of plans and the direction of classes in the training school.

Special Courses for Supervisors of Music, Drawing and for Normal Instructors in State High Schools

The Normal schools have in contemplation the establishing of a special course for those who wish to become teachers of drawing, music, or supervisors of Normal training departments in state high schools. The State Normal Board has asked the Normal Presidents to outline such courses for consideration at its next meeting.

At the time of the preparation of this catalog, however, the courses have not been presented to or approved by the Board. This tentative announcement has been made for the benefit of those who are interested in the proposed work and it will be supplemented by detailed information on application to the President of the school.

CATALOG OF STUDENTS FOR 1911--1912

SPECIAL

Abbott, Kate T.......Paynesville
Fitch, Arthur Leighton..... Haven
Hirt, Edward George....St. Cloud
Ratterman, Anna........St. Paul

Reed, Grace V............Badger
Selke, Wilhelm Erich Sauk Rapids
von Levern, Amelia.....St. Cloud
von Levern, William P., St. Cloud

FIFTH YEAR CLASS

Abel, Clara A...........Shakopee
Aich, Norma.........Minneapolis
Allen, Elsie.............St. Cloud
Anderson, Angeline L., Minneapolis
Anderson, Esther K. ....Willmar
Anderson, Jeanette, Willow River
Askdal, Dora V........Minneota
Barker, Grace M....Minneapolis
Bartz, Lillian Edna...Minneapolis
Bircher, Mary Louise, Minneapolis
Blanchette, Alvena Mary...Anoka
Boehm, Richard ....Pierz
Bonner, Grace Agnes.....Virginia
Brooker, Myrtle C., Frederic, Wis.
Bull, Effie M..............Currie
Bunnell, Iva.........Minneapolis
Campbell, Jos. R., Howard Lake
Castner, Theron S....Minneapolis
Chestek, Abbie..........Hopkins
Chestek, Susan J........Hopkins
Christensen, Ana H., Minneapolis
Coleman, Maude.....Elbow Lake
Collins, Frances M. .....St. Paul
Coughlan, Cecil Mary....St. Cloud
Courtney, Nellie G....Maple Plain
Dahl, Ingga.............St. Cloud
Davey, Irene Pearl.......Eveleth
Dixon, Helen Marie......St. Paul
Dupre, Eva T........White Bear
Dwyer, Eliza..........Monticello

Dwyer, Mary Vivian....Monticello
Eaton, Nellie Ruth.....Elk River
Finn, Beatryce Anna..Minneapolis
Fluke, Helen Frances.....Walker
Foot, Dorothy....Kalispell, Mont.
Gale, John Henry.......St. Cloud
Gallagher, Margaret....St. Cloud
Ghostley, Mabel Grace....Rogers
Gilligan, Frona Anna......Becker
Gould, Herbert B.......St. Cloud
Grimsgard, Edna M. Grove City
Hamar, Nellie............Milaca
Haskell, Mae Belle..South Haven
Hendricks, Lambert M.Watertown
Hewett, Annie...........Soudan
Hodgkin, Cecil Vane.....St. Paul
Holes, Clara...........St. Cloud
Holmberg, Severina C., Beardsley
Hunt, Ellice..............Anoka
Japs, Pearl...........Watertown
Jeffers, Margaret.........Villard
Johnson, Deborah....Minneapolis
Johnson, Myrtle Mae..Cass Lake
Johnstad, Laura Amelia, Glenwood
Jones, Hannah..........St. Paul
Kersten, Minnie M...South Haven
Kleinman, Carrie M...Hutchinson
Krefting, Emma C....Minneapolis
Ladd, Fred Stephen.......Villard
Lange, Millie E......Sauk Centre

Le Vine, Esther F...Marine Mills
Leathers, Blanche L..St. Francis
Lewis, Harriet A.....Minneapolis
Lorentzen, Harriet B.....Willmar
Lund, Mabel C.......Minneapolis
McAlister, Gladys M..Minneapolis
McElroy, Elizabeth......St. Cloud
McShane, Ida Gertrude, Hastings
Malmquist, Myrtle....Minneapolis
Mangan, Helen Irene......Morris
Markley, Jennie.........St. Cloud
Marshik, Frank W..........Pierz
Maybury, Celia Jane....St. Cloud
Mulligan, Anna W........Eveleth
Mulrean, Irene.......Minneapolis
Mumm, Ruth E.....Minneapolis
Munro, Marion..........St. Cloud
Munroe, Gladys E.....Cottonwood
Nelson, Amy Olga........Willmar
Nelson, Ethel Violetta......Afton
Nelson, Ruth Catherine, Elk River
Odell, Mabel Mildred.....Chaska
Olson, Bertha A., Thief River Falls
Oppegaard, Agnes H.....Madison
Parker, Mabel M.....Minneapolis
Poepke, Minnie E.......St. Cloud
Ponsford, Mildred J., Clearwater
Porter, Gertrude A......Willmar
Poston, Sidona, Thief River Falls
Quayle, Mary E.....Moberly, Mo.
Ranney, Helen E.......St. Cloud
Raymond, Cora Marie, St. Cloud
Robbers, Blanche E., Sauk Rapids

Sather, Helen Althea....Willmar
Schweitzer, E. Chippewa Falls, Wis
Shove, Helen Barter, Minneapolis
Sisson, Mattie Estelle.....Dassel
Skibness, Edward J......Benson
Smith, Merle E.........Elk River
Smithson, Beatrice, New London
Sodergren, Helen Irene....Austin
Stanley, Nellie Mae....St. Cloud
Stebbins, Esther, Thief River Falls
Stephenson, Olive I., Long Prairie
Stromme, Minnie O...Minneapolis
Sudheimer, Anna C.....St. Paul
Swanson, Hilma C., Milbank, S. D.
Swenson, Clara E., Centre City
Tarbox, Vivian Ilda....Monticello
Tiedmann, Gertrude R....Melrose
Tolman, Ruth W......Paynesville
Tschumperlin, Rose C., St. Cloud
Turrittin, Mary E....Minneapolis
Upham, Florence E....Monticello
Vale, Gertrude.........St. Cloud
Vogel, Frank............St. Cloud
Walker, Edna.........Alexandria
Webster, Ruby Cora....St. Cloud
Wentland, Paul W....Paynesville
Weyrens, Peter Mathias, St. Cloud
Wheaton, Helen Grace, Elk River
Whitcomb, Anna W......Atwater
White, Roy Winchester, Clearwater
Williams, Anna Matilda, St. Cloud
Wood, Archie Fay....Grey Eagle
Young, Ada Viola....Minneapolis

FOURTH YEAR CLASS

Abbott, G. Albert.....Paynesville
Abrahamson, Ruth A., Buffalo Lake
Alexander, Isabel W....Rockville
Allen, Katie H......Sauk Centre
Alseen, Myrtle F.....Minneapolis

Anderson, Blanche..West St. Paul
Anderson, Caroline Amelia, Mora
Anderson, Elsie Ruth, Minneapolis
Anderson, Freda E......Princeton
Anderson, Lillian E....Kerkhoven

Anderson, Nora Estella, Starbuck
Anderson, Olga C........Atwater
Andrews, Sara Pearl...Alexandria
Angel, Nettie M........Brainerd
Arnson, P.....Michigamme, Mich.
Askdal, Ellen..........Minneota
Barskey, Esther M......St. Cloud
Bartelson, Huldah...Fergus Falls
Bartholomew, Ethel.........Avon
Batz, Hannah Leona......Albany
Beedy, Ruth E........Monticello
Bell, Marian Anne........Glencoe
Bennewitz, Minnie M....Royalton
Benson, Emma S.........Renville
Berg, Lajla, D., Lake Preston, S. D.
Bergman, Oscar Bernard....Foley
Bertelson, Bertha V.....Litchfield
Biddle, Ethel G........Kerkhoven
Biddle, Mae Idella.....Kerkhoven
Bixby, Violet Doris......Kimball
Bowing, Irwin..........St. Cloud
Bradley, Hettie May..Little Falls
Brazil, Angeline.....Minneapolis
Brown, Eunice Alma....Shakopee
Bull, Alta Ruth.........St. Cloud
Burgess, Ethel Estella.....Tower
Burke, Emily...........Waverly
Burke, Margaret Louise, Waverly
Cairney, Edith Loretta....Morris
Carlson, Arthur.........St Cloud
Carlson, Esther Mathilda, Harris
Carlson, Grace.........Brainerd
Carney, Loretta M....Minneapolis
Carney, Olive..........Litchfield
Carpenter, Mamie D., Sauk Rapids
Carr, Pearl Iva...........Alborn
Carter, Helen Clark....St. Cloud
Caylor, Leslie Richard...Kimball
Chalgren, Birdie E., Sauk Rapids
Christianson, Edith V., Stillwater
Clifton, Olive Leona, Sauk Rapids
Compton, Ruth Lucile, Sauk Centre

Cormier, Mayme Margaret, Argyle
Cosens, Lulu Lenore......Hallock
Covart, Hazel E..........Buffalo
Crouley, Hazel K.....Litchfield
Cyrus, Leonard A..Howard Lake
Dahlof, Beda Emelia......Hallock
Dailey, Frances..........Duluth
Daley, Maude Julia...Maple Lake
Dally, Leila Claire.......Laporte
Danforth, Laurel G......St. Cloud
De Haven, Helen F..Minneapolis
Devenney, Katherine G., Shakopee
Dewey, Dessie Ruby, Little Falls
Doherty, Mary.............Osseo
Doten, Fay............Little Falls
Doyle, Alice Genevieve.....Anoka
Doyle, Cecilia D........St. Cloud
Dugan, Grace Isabel....Princeton
Dugas, Mabel..........Cass Lake
Dunnom, Minnie J.......Madison
Dushek, Esther Marie.....Morris
Edmonds, Anne E.........Morris
Egan, Nora Clare.....Minneapolis
Erickson, Carvel E.....Minneota
Erickson, Reiden.....Minneapolis
Evans, Florence V....Clearwater
Farnham, Eva Lavina....Madison
Fessler, William M........Marble
Folmer, Mary C.....Sauk Centre
Fraser, Ella..........Sauk Centre
Fratzke, Pauline E....Hutchinson
Frizelle, Harriette, Parkers Prairie
Gallagher, Louise Isabel...Benson
Gallup, Ina C.............Anoka
Gilberson, Nellie Viola....Ceylon
Ginzel, George August....Ruthton
Gissler, Alvina Erica.......Bruno
Gleeson, Marie........Beardsley
Goff, Katherine Theresa, Litchfield
Gooch, Estelle M......Ellsworth
Gould, Jessamine.........Bemidji
Gould, Roy H..........St. Cloud

Gracie, Estella Cathryn...Bemidji
Gray, Grace Anna.......Wheaton
Green, Florence International Falls
Greenhalgh, Jessie M., Sauk Rapids
Gregory, Walter F......St. Cloud
Groebe, Anna T......Minneapolis
Hagestande, Gena........Madelia
Hagquist, Hulda O., Sauk Rapids
Hallberg, John G......St. Cloud
Hammond, M., San Francisco, Cal.
Hansen, Gertrude Marial, St. Paul
Hanson, Edna Inanda.......Cyrus
Hanson, Mattie C........Stewart
Hanson, Nora M......Hutchinson
Harding, Ruth Alice....Cass Lake
Harker, Eva May........Appleton
Hayden, Florence Helen, Elk River
Hill, Grace Evelyn......Elk River
Hirt, Helen G.........St. Cloud
Hoglund, Alice C........Willmar
Hoglund, Amelia H.........Foley
Holmberg, Frances Othlia, St. Paul
Holmes, Ruth Willard, Glenwood
Hunter, Aileen............Akeley
Hurd, Maude E.........Wabasha
Isaacson, Olive Grace....Madison
Jacobson, A., Abercrombie, N. D.
Johnson, Edith Adeline, Princeton
Johnson, Edward F......Brandon
Johnson, Elizabeth......Franklin
Johnson, Ella Stefania...Minneota
Johnson, Emma Elizabeth, Wadena
Johnson, Esther Gerda......Mora
Johnson, Olga Elizabeth, St. Cloud
Jude, Mabel Clare....Maple Lake
Kaufmann, Martin........Watkins
Kellogg, Treva Goldwood, Royalton
Kendall, Alice H........St. Cloud
Kenneally, Mary T...Minneapolis
Kerlanski, Samuel ......St. Cloud
Kirk, Archie W......Clearwater
Kirkebon, Clara O....Little Falls

Knutsen, Lily..........St. Cloud
Kobe, Helena J.........Royalton
Kochendorfer, Hazel, South Park
Konzen, Gladys Ione......Hallock
Korista, Amanda E., Silver Lake
Korista, Martha L., Silver Lake
Korista, May M......Silver Lake
Korstad, Eline..............Boyd
Kuefler, Hubert......Lake George
Lakin, Ella Frances.....Royalton
Larson, A. Viola.........St. Cloud
Larson, Alice Julia......St. Cloud
Larson, Cora Irene..Fergus Falls
Larson, Hilda Emelia, Sauk Rapids
Larson, Josephine.....Georgeville
Laughton, Bertha M...Clearwater
Lausted, Alice.........St. Cloud
Lende, Rebecca.......Cottonwood
Leopard, Brand........St. Cloud
Ley, Ethel (Ehrlich)....St. Cloud
Libert, John Nicholas...St. Cloud
Lien, Ruth G........Granite Falls
Long, Helen Morgan, Little Falls
Longfellow, Margaret, Monticello
Love, Frances Vera......Big Lake
Lovell, Leona Mildred, St. Cloud
McBride, Margaret W., Elk River
McCauley, Isabel M., Minneapolis
McClay, Frances W.......Cloquet
McCracken, Iva Earl....Princeton
McCrea, Viola C.....Sauk Rapids
McDermott, Winifred.....Clontarf
McDonald, Mary.........Eveleth
McElroy, Arthur........St. Cloud
McGenty, Alice.........St. Cloud
McLachlan, Frances E., Glenwood
McLear, Hattie M....Minneapolis
Maetzold, Bertha F.....Litchfield
Magnell, Bertha Viola, St. Cloud
Mahoney, Madeline V.....Stewart
Maker, Grace, Michigamme, Mich.
Malan, Katherine E.........Ada

Mallay, Gertrude A...Hutchinson
Martini, Loretta Mary, Sauk Rapids
Mathews, Mary Eleanor, Benson
May, Eulalia M........St. Cloud
Maybury, Lenora.......St. Cloud
Maybury, Mary Margaret, St. Cloud
Maynard, Madge L., Long Prairie
Maynard, Winifred, Long Prairie
Mecusker, Marjory....Little Falls
Merwin, Anna Melissa....Wadena
Metlie, Bertha C.......Starbuck
Miller, Lucile.............Osakis
Mills, Annabel...........Bemidji
Mingo, Vera G., Red Beach, Me.
Mitchell, Eva May.....Swanville
Moffet, Minnie E....Minneapolis
Mokros, Fred W.........Bowlus
Molloy, Edith M....Howard Lake
Montgomery, Mayme Jane, Buffalo
Moore, Alice M..........Milaca
Morrison, Ronald Hall....Morris
Morse, Helen.............Mora
Murn, Thomas Joseph.....Parent
Murphy, Ellen Agnes.....Morris
Myron, Afra N. C.......Glenwood
Myron, Mabelle........Glenwood
Nehring, Rhoda H....Paynesville
Nelson, Magda..........Wendell
Norgaard, Paula G., Granite Falls
North, Therza, Sierre Madre, Cal.
Notton, Lois G.......Little Falls
O'Connor, Edna J........Renville
O'Maley, Thomas Walter, St. Cloud
Oberg, Hildred I....Minneapolis
Oberg, J. Ross.........St. Cloud
Oberg, Mabel........Minneapolis
Olson, Nicoline C..........Cyrus
Olson, Olaf............McIntosh
Palmer, Hazel Eileen, Little Falls
Peifer, Lena Magdalen, Litchfield
Perkins, Cluda A.....Annandale
Perkins, Edith Carrie...St. Cloud

Perkins, Florence G.....Donnelly
Perrault, Charlotte K., Cass Lake
Perrault, Elizabeth....Cass Lake
Petersen, Margaret M......Osseo
Peterson, Bertha E....Big Lake
Peterson, Ethel Adena..St. Cloud
Peterson, Hilda Amalia, Hinckley
Podall, Daniel A.....Wood Lake
Pote, Hazel...Michigamme, Mich.
Price, Maud Lucile...Minneapolis
Radeck, Mildred A...Minneapolis
Ratterman, Louise.......St. Paul
Robinson, Sherrill E....Kimball
Roos, Alma A.........Princeton
Rudd, Ida Theodora......Flaming
Ryan, Eva Elizabeth....Royalton
Ryan, Margaret Irene....Staples
Ryan, Sarah Leonilla....St. Cloud
Sander, Alma R.......Lindstrom
Sargent, Bessie Lenore....Osakis
Sartell, Mildred E.......Sartell
Sather, Arnold A., Eau Claire, Wis.
Schmidt, Edward........Belgrade
Schmidt, Rose.........St. Cloud
Schroeder, Angela R.....Perham
Schwegman, Joseph..Sauk Centre
Scott, John Frederic....St. Cloud
Selke, Arthur Carl..Sauk Rapids
Selke, George A....Sauk Rapids
Sell, Myrtle E........Monticello
Shattuck, Jessie.......Clearwater
Shean, Nelle Agnes......Sparta
Sholund, Anna...........Eveleth
Simons, Mary Elizabeth..Bemidji
Simpson, Anna Eloise....Hewitt
Sjoberg, Alice C.......Royalton
Skoglund, Jennie M....Clara City
Slattengren, Hattie E., Lindstrom
Slawson, Vera Pearl......Morris
Sliter, Beatrice E.,...Minneapolis
Soderman, Luella.........Dassel
Stangl, Fred H........St. Cloud

Stanley, Dora...........Kimball
Steiner, Ida Emilie..........Echo
Stenger, Regina Theresa..Morris
Stewart, Donald........St. Cloud
Stromgren, Ruth E., Centre City
Styner, M. Louise....Maple Plain
Swadling, Clio Delphine...Milaca
Swenson, Annie........Smithville
Thompson, Beulah E., Elk River
Trengove, Florence M..McKinley
Tschumperlin, Anna K..St. Cloud
Vale, Bernice ....St. Cloud
Wagner, Lola L...........Becker
Warczak, Stephania..Minto, N. D.

Weidner, Rose B.....Minneapolis
Welder, Maude Elizabeth....Delhi
Wesseler, Gail...............
....Victoria de las Tunas, Cuba
Wheeler, Dorothy J......Norwood
Wieland, Bessie........Brainerd
Williams, Dora Vivian......Mora
Williams, Sigfred Gust..St. Cloud
Wing, Helen Frances....St. Cloud
Winkelman, Bernard G.....Foley
Woodcock, Lydia A.....Princeton
Wright, Florence E......St. Cloud
Ziegler, Walter E.....Brook Park

THIRD YEAR CLASS

Abell, Walter..........St. Cloud
Allen, Mildred Joy......St. Cloud
Anderson, V. Lillian L., Lindstrom
Arndt, Sadie Mable......St. Cloud
Beatty, Florence Helen..St. Cloud
Benson, Agnes E., Chisago City
Berg, Herman........Forest City
Bernick, Carola G..Cold Springs
Blair, Grace Rebecca....Glenwood
Brisson, Martha.........Virginia
Bruns, Lillian A........Donnelly
Buckman, Phoebe.......St. Cloud
Burns, Agnes K.....Sauk Rapids
Calhoun, Sara Mae......Randall
Calkin, Helen E....Minneapolis
Cameron, Abbie Gail, Sauk Rapids
Carlson, Lillian C.....Clear Lake
Casey, Alice Frances, Minneapolis
Cater, Mabel, Estelle....St. Cloud
Caylor, Edna Esther.....Kimball
Clark, Guy Wheeler.....St. Cloud
Collin, Mary T.....Sacred Heart
Courtney, Rose M.....St. Cloud
Davis, Fred E..........Gemmell

Dreis, Ursula T......St. Augusta
Dunn, Margaret Mary...St. Cloud
Erickson, Clara Hilma...St. Cloud
Evans, Marguerite L..Clearwater
Everest, Nellie Gertrude.Brainerd
Farris, Margaret Fidelia..Becker
Ferdinantsen, Charlotte, St. Cloud
Flynn, Ethel Mae.....Clearwater
Fuglie, Christine..........Ashby
Gaumnitz, Caroline...Minneapolis
Gregory, Ida Minerva......Haven
Griffith, Mae........St. Vincent
Griffith, Margaret E...St. Vincent
Hagberg, Nimle A......St. Cloud
Hallberg, Esther........St. Cloud
Hanlon, Alma..........St. Cloud
Hansen, Ella S.........Bertram
Hegne, Rose............Barrett
Hoftoe, Rowena Amanda....Nevis
Houghton, Harriet F.....Kimball
Jenkins, Mildred E...Minneapolis
Jensen, Marie...........St. Paul
Johnson, Agnes I........Haven
Johnson, Esther..Red Lake Falls

A VIEW IN NEW GYMNASIUM

MODEL BUILDING

A RECITATION ROOM

Johnson, Florence Emily, St. Cloud
Johnson, Victor Axel....St. Cloud
Juergens, Ella L........St. Cloud
Keohen, Mary E.....Montgomery
Kline, Mabel Claire..Pine River
Koch, Mae Elizabeth....St. Cloud
Kuefler, Barney.....Lake George
Kuehn, Ernest Fred ....St. Cloud
Lee, Clara ....Cyrus
Lindell, Ellen Mathilda....Harris
Long, Paulina...........Wheaton
Lorenz, Edith A.........Akeley
Lundeen, Eleanor.....Lindstrom
Lyman, Ruth, B....Redwood Falls
Mankenberg, C. F., Young America
Murphy, Martha M.....St. Cloud
Nelson, Aurora F.....Forest Lake
Newton, Wenonah B....St. Cloud
Nygaard, Borghild A....Starbuck
O'Rourke, Timothy....Annandale
Oliver, Florence G......St. Cloud
Omundson, Mabel Ruth..St. Cloud
Osterberg, Florence M....Farwell
Paquette, Peter Martin....Darwin
Parent, Josephine A.....Parent
Payne, Inez Lillian....Wood Lake
Pennie, Alma, Fair Acres, Canada
Peterson, Emily, Parkers Prairie
Porter, Lavina.......Centre City
Preice, Rosa B.........St. Cloud
Randall, Cotter........St. Cloud
Rankin, Nellie R........Badger
Robertson, Marie G....Princeton
Rolighed, Olena Elsie...Appleton

Ryan, Sadie Caroline..St. Vincent
Scanlon, Mary S.....Maple Lake
Schellinger, Otto Peter..St. Cloud
Schmitt, Martin J.........Avon
Schutt, Jennie Dorothea, St. Cloud
Scott, Laura E............Foley
Severance, Lila E......Princeton
Shea, Frances Theresa...Garfield
Skjeveland, Valdina, Hanley Falls
Smith, Ethel Emily, Rangely, Col.
Smith, Mildred.........St. Cloud
Smithson, Flossie E..New London
Spangrud, Emelia.......Starbuck
Sperley, Bertha Johanna, Verndale
Stark, Ida Vahlborg.....St. Cloud
Storey, Gertrude Mae........Ada
Stuart, Rena............Laporte
Stubbs, Winifred C.....St. Cloud
Terry, Dassie L...Parkers Prairie
Thompson, Cora F........Badger
Thompson, Helen E....Princeton
Tonnell, Beda Gertrude..St. Cloud
Tonnell, Eleanor........St. Cloud
Turner, Guy Ernest......Kimball
Turnquist, Hannah E..Kerkhoven
Voss, Ida Amelia......Bellingham
White, Marian Frances...Bemidji
Wicklem, Eleanor........St. Paul
Williams, Donnie........St. Cloud
Wimmer, Nanita ....Albany
Wold, Bertha M........Princeton
Wright, Myra Kathryne..St. Cloud
Zack, Anna..............St. Cloud

SECOND YEAR CLASS

Anderson, Ellen C. E....Kennedy
Anderson, Esther E....Big Lake
Anderson, Ethel J.....Belgrade
Anderson, Laura A.......Randall

Anderson, Ruth E....Waite Park
Archibald, Florence E..Deerwood
Barnum, Zay...........St. Cloud
Barr, Clarence.........St. Cloud

Barthelemy, Susan M.....Minden
Bartling, Emma.........Brainerd
Barton, Lillian..........St. Cloud
Bengtson, Henry P....Paynesville
Bergman, Frieda C.........Foley
Biddle, Lorena Grace..Kerkhoven
Borman, H...Abercrombie, N. D..
Bremer, Freda Elizabeth.Waverly
Brennan, Clara Mae......Minden
Broecker, Lena Amelia.....Copas
Brommenschenkel, A.Sauk Centre
Brooks, Maud Alma.......Becker
Bruener, Albert L......St. Cloud
Campbell, Irene Gladys...Randall
Campbell, Ray M........St. Cloud
Carey, Ruth Rachel.....St. Cloud
Carlson, Ruth Theresia..St. Cloud
Carpenter E........Sauk Rapids
Cater, Pearl L.......Sauk Rapids
Christenson, Lena.....Deerwood
Cipala, George........Holdingford
Clark, Myrtle M......Grey Eagle
Dickerman, Lillian I...Marshall
Disselkamp, Aurelia K..Hoffman
Donovan, Mary B.........Foley
Drexler, Mamie.......Millerville
Dunnewold, May Edna...St. Cloud
Dwyer, Alice R......Clear Lake
Edwards, Edna Lucile..Swanville
Ehlers, Marie............Wadena
Engbloom, Edith L.....Elk River
Erickson, Agnes E......St. Cloud
Ernst, Anna..............Danvers
Eshpeter, Anna.........Rockville
Fish, Hazel V..........St. Cloud
Fitzpatrick, Daniel......St. Cloud
Friedman, Frances O.Eden Valley
Gannon, Ambrose D.......Sedan
Ganzer, Gertrude Elis..Richmond
Glass, Adella Anna......St. Cloud
Godbout, Rose Mary..Eden Valley
Graham, Mary H...Sauk Centre

Graham, Nellie V.......Melrose
Grandstrand, Addie M..Lindstrom
Grant, Mary J......Sauk Rapids
Gray, Lillian E.........St. Cloud
Grimes, Margaret E...Grey Eagle
Guy, George............St. Cloud
Hall, J. Kathleen......St. Cloud
Hanrahan, Julia..........Morris
Harris, Helen Dorothy..St. Cloud
Haselkamp, Hattie A....St. Cloud
Henry, Stella A...........Foley
Herman, Anna A.........Gilman
Herman, Clara Marie ....Gilman
Hilder, Bertha Louise...St. Cloud
Hilder, Molly Esther....St. Cloud
Hollern, Dorothy L.....St. Cloud
Holt, Stella Pauline.......Spicer
Inman, Stella M......Eden Valley
Jacobson, G...Abercrombie, N. D.
Johnson, Anna E....Moose Lake
Kalkman, Louise M...Clear Lake
Keefe, Cora E..........Ronneby
Keefe, Josie...............Foley
Kiley, Erma A.......Holdingford
Knight, Edyth May...Montevideo
Knott, Effie L..........Raymond
Koelzer, Frances Anna...Watkins
Kolbet, Leonard............Rice
Krause, Martha Bertha......Rice
Krebs, Rosalie O........St. Cloud
Lahr, Rose S............St. Cloud
Lahr, Susan........Eden Valley
Lake, Charles J........Richmond
Lane, Estella.............Anoka
Larsen, Inez M..........St. Cloud
Lee, Jennie Elizabeth....Farwell
Leitch, Luella...........Freeport
Lemm, Ignatius.........St. Cloud
Liljedahl, Mabel E......St. Cloud
Lyons, Blanche A....South Haven
McKee, Helena.........Kennedy
Merrick, Frank Alford.......Kent

Mitchell, Mary C.......St. Cloud
Mockenhaupt, Frances..St. Cloud
Moe, Martin..Abercrombie, N. D.
Moe, William..Abercrombie, N. D.
Molitor, Marie E........Belgrade
Momburg, Rose Marie.......Rice
Moog, Julia Theresa..Sauk Rapids
Murphy, Kathryn M.......Morris
Murphy, Lucy Ellen....St. Cloud
Murray, Mayme E.........Foley
Nelson, Agnes J.....Chisago City
Norman, Ragnhild........Milaca
O'Brien, Alice Mary..Eden Valley
Olsson, Edna M.........Brandon
Pallansch, Mayme C.....Albany
Parent, Anna E..........Parent
Parent, Della E..........Parent
Parent, Ethel T...........Foley
Peterson, Esther J......Garfield
Peterson, Marande.......Barrett
Quayle, Sarah Jane..Moberly, Mo.
Rajkowski, Helen...........Rice
Rankin, Jessie Laird.....Badger
Raymond, Lloyd Leland...Becker
Reed, Helen Elizabeth..Raymond
Reiter, Catherine E...Waite Park
Richard, Mary M.........Haven
Rockwood, Malcolm.....St. Cloud
Rose, Nellie M.........St. Cloud
Ross, Hazel Esther.....St. Cloud
Ross, Julia Lorean......St. Cloud
Rourke, Maggie K.........Foley
Rourke, Mary Ellen........Foley
Rystedt, Alice...........Farwell
Schey, Emma Marie......Argyle
Schmitz, Nicholas.......Belgrade

Schommer, Celia R..Eden Valley
Schommer, Margaret..Eden Valley
Schreiner, Adeline......Litchfield
Schuoler, Eleanor...........Rice
Schutt, Minnie M......St. Cloud
Schwalier, Anna M...Little Falls
Sigloh, Maybelle Eola...St. Cloud
Smith, Frankie Louise.....Harris
Smithson, Katie.....New London
Smithson, May I....New London
Speiser, Elizabeth......St. Joseph
Speiser, Ida E........St. Joseph
Spoden, John M......Paynesville
Stickney, Anna Lydia....Kimball
Stoughton, Catherine E....Fisher
Streitz, Clara V........St. Cloud
Swanson, Harry........St. Cloud
Thompson, Myrtle F....Brandon
Thorn, Samuel A.........Becker
Tipton, Gladys..............Avon
Towne, Charlie Earl........Foley
Tschida, John L.........Freeport
Tschida, Michael F......Freeport
Vitalis, Vendla M.........Shafer
Vogel, John Willard....St. Cloud
Vos, Clara...............Albany
Wagner, Beulah G........Becker
Walters, Lillie Artolia..St. Cloud
Webster, Zuella...........Fisher
Wesseler, Carrie..............
....Victoria de las Tunas, Cuba
Widman, Rose Johanna.....Avon
Williams, Leonard......St. Cloud
Witzman, Susan.........Watkins
Wolhart, Effie Celestia.......Rice
Wolhart, Willard H..........Rice

FIRST YEAR CLASS

Agather, Theodora L..Sauk Rapids
Ames, Maude Ellen.......Guthrie
Andersen, Nannie...Sauk Centre

Anderson, Anna Marie...Brainerd
Anderson, Clara C.....Princeton
Anderson, Leslie H.....St. Cloud

Anderson, Lydia E........Carlos
Anderson, Ruth E........Carlos
Apmann, Selma Bertha....Haven
Arbo, Elsie Jane.........Ogilvie
Arbo, Olive I.............Ogilvie
Arndt, Vera L.........St. Cloud
Asher, Leila...........St. Cloud
Atkinson, Marjorie E.....Duane
Backlund, Olga Carolyn..Hoffman
Barry, Chester Daniel.Grey Eagle
Bartling, Ellen E.......Brainerd
Beach, Stella D.....Callao, Peru
Bechtel, Hilda M......St. Joseph
Beltz, Marguerite Julia...St. Paul
Berg, Hildegard, S....Lindstrom
Beste, Andrew............Osakis
Bjorklund, Madelaine V..St. Cloud
Blattner, Roy W........St. Cloud
Bloomquist, Edward E.....Copas
Boldan, Glee Jennie...Clearwater
Boobar, Eliza H.............Nary
Boos, Francis..........St. Cloud
Brakke, Minnie G.........Milroy
Brandvick, Skulfrid C......Nary
Brick, Othmar Philip....St. Cloud
Briggs, Carrie Mae.......Motley
Britton, Linea Haidee.....Motley
Brown, Margaret M.....St. Cloud
Burr, Laura Christine...Marshall
Burrows, Florence E..Deer Creek
Buttweiler, Mathilda.....Melrose
Cain, Myrtle...........Brainerd
Calhoun, Rosalie Frances..Randall
Campbell, Harold Arthur.St. Cloud
Carew, LuElla Genevieve.Wadena
Carey, Eva M.........St. Cloud
Carpenter, James H..Sauk Rapids
Casey, Helen G.....Sauk Rapids
Casey, Kathleen V...Sauk Rapids
Cater, Ray Frederick...St. Cloud
Cedergren, Emma L.North Branch
Chaika, Mary..........St. Cloud

Chapman, Gertrude......St. Cloud
Cheeseman, Margaret J...Barnum
Christianson, Runa......Minneota
Clark, Bacil Harland..Grey Eagle
Clark, Carol Harriet.....St. Cloud
Clark, Glen Haddy....Grey Eagle
Collins, Ethel F.....Sauk Centre
Collver, Minnie Clare.....Carlton
Cook, Cora A...........Brainerd
Cousin, Viola E.........Bemidji
Dadie, Alice........Minneapolis
Daehn, Ida A..............Foley
Dally, Lois Elizabeth....Laporte
Dandanell, Esther E......Nisswa
Danlake, Hattie A.........Foley
Danzl, Rose Catherine..St. Cloud
Davis, Belle.............Randall
Davis, Cora.............Randall
Day, Edith..........Minneapolis
Dobbdal, Arla Ruth.......Guthrie
Dobbdal, Norma Juliette..Guthrie
Donovan, Josephine C.....Foley
Dorenkamper, Lizzie....Lismore
Dorenkamper, Mary......Lismore
Doyle, Gladys Carola....St. Cloud
Dunnewold, John........St. Cloud
Dwyer, Lauretta C.....Santiago
Eastman, Edna Isabel..Big Lake
Eaton, Grace M..........Arago
Ekblad, Euricka......Evansville
Elgren, Andy C.......St. Cloud
Elkjer, Thora A........Pennock
Emilson, Sophia........Brainerd
Enderle, Hugo A........Watkins
Engen, Stina.............Sebeka
Erickson, Ruth E.....Waite Park
Faust, Cresence............Pierz
Ferguson, Clara E.......Staples
Fiskerbeck, Georgia......Brooten
Freeberg, Esther Elvira..St. Cloud
Freed, John............St. Cloud
Friese, John Frank......St. Cloud

Fuchs, Lidwina E......St. Cloud
Fuhrman, Laura.........Johnson
Gaffney, Laura...........Morris
Gannon, Mae.............Sedan
Ganzer, Mary.........Richmond
Gasper, Albert E.........Watkins
Gatrell, Gladys G......St. Cloud
Gaumnitz, Walter...........Rice
Gerding, Anna..........Melrose
Gerding, Veronica E.....Melrose
Gerrie, Bernice.......Cedarbend
Gilchrist, Elvie S.........Buffalo
Gilchrist, Harriet A...Monticello
Gladen, May............Laporte
Goetten, Andrew Wilbur.St. Cloud
Goltz, John C.............Gilman
Green, Mabel...........Ruthton
Grondin, Fern..........Brainerd
Grossman, Julietta......St. Cloud
Gruber, Leone.........St. Cloud
Guthrie, Jeanette.......St. Cloud
Hallberg, Luella........St. Cloud
Hansen, Marie Louise...St. Cloud
Hanson, Olga E..........Ogilvie
Harris, Jennie Irene..Fort Ripley
Hartel, Edith V.........St. Cloud
Hartel, George T......St. Cloud
Hartel, O'Tilla Kate....St. Cloud
Hedin, Minnie A....Norway Lake
Henderson, Alice Mary....Nisswa
Hibbard, Jesse E......St. Cloud
Hiller, Mary.........St. Francis
Hines, Jennie L.....Sauk Centre
Hines, Marguerite G..Sauk Centre
Hingsberger, Helen A..St. Cloud
Hinman, Elma Irene..Grey Eagle
Hollern, Margeret..Sauk Rapids
Hosford, Ione Ellen......Marshall
Huber, Genevieve E....St. Cloud
Huebner, Jeanette......St. Cloud
Hursh, Ina Isabel........Henning
Huseth, Olive............Barrett

Jaenson, Harold Albert..St. Cloud
Jenkins, Beth..........St. Cloud
Jernberg, Ruth Dorothy.St. Cloud
Johnson, Ebba H........Atkinson
Johnson, Elvira Augusta, Harrell
Johnson, Emma C......Marietta
Jude, Lena E........Maple Lake
Kalkmann, Flora M...Clear Lake
Kamp, Catherine A....Richmond
Kane, Anna Belle....Sauk Centre
Kanthak, Antonia.........Nassau
Katzmarek, Helen A..Holdingford
Kay, Gertrude C.....Little Falls
Kellogg, Anna..........Royalton
Kiernan, Mary A........Watkins
Kimball, Celia C.....Fort Ripley
Kjelstrup, Norman.......Hoffman
Knight, Bessie E.....Montevideo
Knudson, Alma Christine, Ausland
Kobler, Leona M.....Deer Creek
Koehler, Elizabeth M...St. Cloud
Koltes, Mary R.........Norcross
Kornann, Dora..............Avon
Korn, Alice M.......Clara City
Korn, Lydia R.........Clara City
Kravig, Lillian Regina...Renville
Kreisel, Cora Antoinette....Boyd
Krieg, Elfa C..........St. Cloud
Krueger, Lydia W....Little Falls
Kuiper, Katie.........Clara City
Kurlunski, Fanny......St. Cloud
Lahr, Louise E.........St. Cloud
Lahr, Susanna M........Le Sauk
Landa, Myrtle..........Brandon
Landeen, Lillian.........Brandon
Landwehr, John W......St. Cloud
Lapham, Nellie Irene......Anoka
Larson, Alma J.........Belgrade
Larson, Ellen Bernadine.St. Cloud
Larson, Florence M....Alexandria
Larson, Lillian........Littlefork
Larson, Margaret A....Cass Lake

Leaf, Bessie........Forest Lake
Leary, Loretta............Easton
Lemm, Dominick........St. Cloud
Lentz, Lulu M...........Wadena
Lindberg, Hilma Maria.Sandstone
Litchy, Mae.............St. Cloud
Little, Irma..............Melrose
Liveringhouse, Fannie.....Ramey
Lowell, Edna M........Princeton
Luckeroth, Anna M......Albany
Lunde, Anna.........Lintonville
Lundstrom, Earl Edwin...Garfield
Lyddon, Nelly..........Brainerd
Lynch, Mary S.........Foreston
McCormick, Cecilia.....St. Cloud
McCormick, Elizabeth D...Haven
McGowan, Mary E....Grey Eagle
McGuire, Rebecca.........Foley
McKenzie, Mattie Edith..St. Cloud
McNeely, Mary Alice....St. Cloud
McQueen, Leigh.......St. Cloud
Mahoney, Mary Regina..Faribault
Malan, Frances..............Ada
Marget, Verna E..........Isanti
Markley, Alice Barbara, St. Cloud
Matthews, Inez Ruby......Anoka
Matthies, Lucy.......Alexandria
Maybury, Avisia........St. Cloud
Meyer, Anna.................Pierz
Meyer, Margaret C........Pierz
Meyer, Theresa C.........Pierz
Mies, Mary Annie........Watkins
Modahl, Alice........Alexandria
Moe, Celeste Louise.....Ronneby
Moe, Margarette B........Loman
Mooney, Mary J.....Sauk Rapids
Morgan, James L.....Holdingford
Morgan, Mabel E.....Holdingford
Morrison, Ruth C.........Copas
Moser, Henry M......Eden Valley
Mudd, Neva...........Sandstone
Murn, Medora Frances...Ronneby

Murphy, Wellington..Holdingford
Murray, Jesse James...St. Cloud
Mutschler, Albert......St. Cloud
Myers, Margaret E......Murdock
Nelson, Anna...........Wendell
Nelson, Flossie Loretta.....Afton
Nelson, Helen M........St. Cloud
Nelson, Mary E......Grove City
Ness, Eunice Cecelia....St. Cloud
Neuman, Elizabeth.........Pierz
Nichols, Leah Madge..Alexandria
Nilson, Lydia E.....Holdingford
Nolting, Clara.......Park Rapids
O'Brien, Mary Frances....Becker
Oberley, Grace Ruth....St. Cloud
Odegaard, Alma Elizabeth, Sebeka
Odegaard, Josephine H....Sebeka
Oliver, Lorimer.........St. Cloud
Olmscheid, John.........Melrose
Olson, David Renhold....St. Cloud
Olson, Ernest.......... St. Cloud
Olson, Ida Goldie.....Crow Wing
Opheim, Herbert Jerome...Cyrus
Orgon, Lauretta Mae....St. Cloud
Orgon, Mae Agnes...... St. Cloud
Osborne, A. Fingal........Milaca
Ostergren, Hannah......St. Cloud
Palmer, Grace Gertrude..Brainerd
Parent, Helen A..........Parent
Parent, Lena Belle........Parent
Parish, Irene Hazel.....St. Cloud
Parmeter, Viva............Loman
Pearson, Elida..........St. Cloud
Pelton, Sadie B......Sauk Rapids
Pentin, Lena Emily......Brainerd
Perlowski, Frnces T..Sauk Rapids
Perlowski, Minnie C..Sauk Rapids
Peterson, Edith C...Willow River
Peterson, Mabel J.....Pine River
Peterson, Sarah A......Deerwood
Phelps, Maude I........Brainerd
Pilson, Almeda......Long Prairie

Pitzl, Anna L........New Munich
Porwoll, Marie.........St. Cloud
Quigley, Gertrude Mary..Danvers
Randall, Mary Eleanor..St. Cloud
Ranney, Marguerite M..St. Cloud
Ranstedt, Ellen J........Hoffman
Rassier, Stella C.....St. Joseph
Rassier, Susan Bertha..St. Joseph
Rausch, John...............Zions
Reed, Ruth A. H........Almelund
Rengel, Stella M.......St. Cloud
Ritter, Rose Mary..........Avon
Rode, Kathryn...........Hewitt
Rode, L. Maude..........Hewitt
Roeser, Arnold.........St. Cloud
Ryan, Anna Laura.......Royalton
Saboe, Henrietta........Belgrade
Saboe, Minnie..........Belgrade
Sather, Camilla............Osakis
Salisbury, Marguerite.Eden Valley
Sauter, Bathilda E........Morris
Schiffman, Caroline M...St. Cloud
Schoberg, Anna E...Chisago City
Schoenborn, Michael.....Melrose
Schultheis, Rose V...Holdingford
Schwartz, Martha.Parkers Prairie
Schwartz, Mary C.....Groningen
Senti, Henrietta......Browerville
Shekleton, Marie G.....Murdock
Simons, Ella Edyth..Little Falls
Simons, Florence K.....Randall
Simons, Katherine......Deerwood
Skafte, Myrtle.........St. Cloud
Skejevland, Arthur..Hanley Falls
Skold, Mabel Lillian...Monticello
Smart, Charles H......St. Cloud
Smart, Mabel Ellen.....St. Cloud
Smith, Cecylia May..Little Falls
Snow, Etta Elizabeth.....Ausland
Spangelo, Mabel Margie..Pillager
Spengler, Lucy R.........Melrose
Stack, Dorothy A.........Anoka

Staples, Eva...........St. Joseph
Stenerson, Oscar F....Georgeville
Strandberg, Edith E......Morris
Swanson, Millie..........Bertha
Ten Eyck, Mary Louisa...Quiring
Theisen, Anton..........Watkins
Thompson, Andrew T....Belgrade
Thompson, Eda B....Elbow Lake
Thornton, Myrtle......Pine River
Thorson, Mabel Tina..Maple Plain
Todd, Lora J............Kerrick
Trebiatowski, Julia E..Little Falls
Turner, Bernice C..Spencer Brook
Van Eaton, Carrie........Osakis
Van Eaton, Maud E.......Osakis
Vermilyea, Leo. B.......Verndale
Vermilyea, Mabel Rose..Verndale
Volner, Edna Marie......Staples
Wagner, Clara E.........Bertha
Wahl, Arthur L.........St. Cloud
Wahl, Gertrude C........St. Cloud
Wahl, Wilfred..........St. Cloud
Waite, Frank Arthur.......Haven
Waite, Ida Alice........St. Cloud
Waite, Olive E...........Haven
Walker, Pearl R........St. Cloud
Walbridge, Mabel I........Hewitt
Waligorsky, Helen M....Royalton
Walz, Caroline G......St. Joseph
Warner, Jacoba.........Perham
Weekley, Gladys M..Willow River
Weiland, Hattie H.....Clara City
Weisman, Henry I......Rockville
Welch, Anna J..........Wadena
Wenstrom, Sanford V.Waite Park
Wentland, Edward.Wibaux, Mont.
Weyrens, Elfrieda E.....St. Cloud
Whitcomb, Ethel Gladys.Hancock
Whitten, Jessie Alice...Deerwood
Williams, Stella Louise..St. Cloud
Wilson, Hilda E......Pine River
Wilwerding, Katherine...Freeport

Winings, Josephine M....Watkins
Wozniak, Barbara....Little Falls
Yeo, Jane...............Minneota

Zeck, Theodore.......Holdingford
Zinn, Hazelle M.. ...St. Cloud

RECAPITULATION

NORMAL DEPARTMENT

Graduate Classes:

Senior Graduate Class	109
Junior Graduate Class	201
Elementary Graduate Class	52
	362

Academic Professional Classes:

Senior Class	17
Junior Class	35
Third Year Class	115
Second Year Class	163
First Year Class	347
	677
Special Students	8
	1047

TRAINING DEPARTMENT

Eighth Grade	43
Seventh Grade	26
Sixth Grade	25
Fifth Grade	7
Fourth Grade	15
Third Grade	12
Second Grade	18
First Grade	28
	174

Enrollment, summer term, 1911	548
Enrollment, fall, winter and spring, 1911-1912	614
Graduates of the School, 1911-1912	144

NORMAL BUILDINGS FROM EAST SIDE

VIEW OF TENTH STREET BRIDGE, SOUTH OF CAMPUS